MOODY BLUE

Larry Rochelle

2006

MOODY BLUE

CONTENTS

To the good folks of Kansas who always seem to get it wrong and to the magic of Elvis who continues to excite and inspire, even though he's dead, dead, dead.

Bringing Elvis to Kansas

Placing Elvis Presley in Kansas seems absurd. His rich lifestyle and flamboyant clothing would be sinful in Kansas' small towns and small town thinking would keep him so oppressed. He'd have to escape to avoid being stunted and runted. But Kansas still dreams about Elvis, longs to hear his voice, longs to touch him and hug him.

In spite of this longing, the myth of Kansas being the home of the Wizard of Oz also seems mistaken. The Wizard's home, so glorious and shining, can't be here. Such magic belongs elsewhere. One real-life attempt to bring the Wizard to Kansas as a theme park ended when the land to be purchased turned out to be a weapons range, much too cruel and expensive for the Wizard.

And the bleak Kansas plains seem bereft of support for the adventures of the lion, the tin man and the straw man. Elvis himself, with all his powers, could not find a yellow brick road here; the Kansas legislature would be too cheap to build one.

No, any visit by Elvis must remain in the realm of fantasy. And what better way to bring him to meet the Wizard than through poetry.

Elvis Arrives in Oz

fringe seemed to be
blowing in the wind,
songs were just drops of water
from cyclones criss-crossing the plains,
hopping frogs dropping from the sky.

painted ladies tumbled out of tumbrels
and the Wizard wore his black hat
over one eye, his long gray locks
fishtailing as he moved.

guitars arrived, then musicians,
most heading low into the wind,
put off by bimbos, an entire flock,
blown in from Vegas.

the dark-haired slickness of the stranger's
hair fooled the Wizard
at first, his nimble eyes
fastening on spandex jumpsuits
and pomaded follicles.

an eerie light, greenish and cold,
moved along the plains, and one man
stood under it, his sneer almost like
a smile, but colder, his black hair
reflecting the Apocalypse,
his red cape over his white suit,
his lion belt flashing lightning.

they shook hands and bowed, the Wizard
and the King, working magic under skies
rife with whirling tombs, dodging poisonous snakes
raking the fields.

Moving from Tupelo

next to weather maps
spread outward from oak chairs,
near power pinnacles,
lie orifices of the poor, most
bleeding from blows struck
for hatred, blows too granite-tough
to avoid, night
wounds in the middle of poverty,
votes of constituents blunted by
whispered corridor words,
and nothing counted after all.

Cold Kansas Wind

blessings of gold coins drip
slowly, if at all, down,
down time-lines drawn by snakes,
snakes, only the grass rifts wronged
by lies (too cold for parrots
sleeping through rainbows)
trace stories, whiplashes,
cold earaches brought home
to empty refrigerators
bleeding sour milk.

Dustbowl Fever

No—don't touch the band-aids in
the lower drawer, yes: that one
contains the tepid towels
from last summer's rain,
a cold compress to wipe away
those tears you wept one night,
that June night, so the song said,
when lovers' lips parted
and cicadas blossomed eerily after
that midnight kiss.

Darkening Sky

My wife, Ruth, and I took our first trip through Kansas in the summer of 1967. We crossed the vast Flint Hills and probably listening to Elvis on the radio. We were on our way to an NDEA English Institute in Laramie. Radio stations interrupted the music to warn us about the moist atmosphere, the darkening sky as we traveled I-70 west.

As we neared Goodland ,Kansas, we were amazed at the green, rolling hills and the endless sky. What a beautiful, stark and scary place. At about seven p.m., we turned off the Interstate and found a motel, the air very still. But as we unpacked our bags and went inside ready for rest, the television warned us of twisters nearby. The hotel manager told us to go to the basement. Huddling together with our two young sons, we had to smile. Kansas was proving faithful to our memory of THE WIZARD OF OZ.

Tornado Fear

somehow the concept of green tumbles
rather than rolls and white specks teach
trajectory instantly.
the response of low noise
catches the anger and one
dancer blanches, her eyes reflected by TV
cameras: how could she
forget the distance?
her mother warned her:
the tongue wobbles but
the breast must remain
pure,
the stance wide.
the spectators
turn to watch,
the stagnant pond rippling
to her disgust,
the dancing pole ripped to heaven.

The Kansas Politician

crack-knobbed fingers,
stuck near slit-like pockets,
grasp for apples
knocked to ground by Kansas winds.
the prairie often issues threats,
and clay-hardened figurines shudder,
their stone-brains built
only for statuesque remarks.
the sun hot on ears of clay, the bird
droppings a constant irritant,
waxed memories of flippant remarks
unheard, the icon captures every
glance, every bedazzled bird-song,
and hides them
in a memory too small
for tears.

Blue Moon

grotesquely, descending in paisley shirt
down down past lingering guests,
the habitué stumbles once,
the heft
of ancient dreams budding
once again, unencumbered by
alcohol now, but dumbing-down
slightly, each effort to face the
white orb a demented failure,
each salute to friends
dampened instantly, and no one
near to catch his hand or hold him
closer after last night's
disappointment.

Neon Sunflowers

not my favorite flower
but one spread about in fantasy by
grave-diggers hoping for fuel
to light their enigmas.

each sky light glows danger,
flows monsters, each step brings
melancholy to the scene,
and creatures seem poised now,

running in circles,
round and round oak trees,
planted to attract moss, that green
spreading downwards toward
tombs unopened by moons,
unwanted by the gods.

Night Gig

webbed-feet fevered with incessant
desires track the tonsils of rats, who,
urged out of holes too deep
for men to fathom, clutch at lost
diamonds and snag the souls of sinners,
each creature using slow-motion photography
to ensure fame, no fortune coming
to the rat-faced clowns, but the video
trail will show how they
lived, how they fought.

Flea Market Blues

mostly horizontal, the singer's
croon leaned into melody, causing
passersby to knock knees on abruptly
hyphenated table legs
with brown mahogany stain still wet
between the leaves.

the course of stopped traffic pushed
pedestrians into galvanized sculptures, each one
resting its head on slightly skewed
water colors.

the domino effect lingered after dark,
musicians miffed by candied
apples stuck to ersatz ivy, tracing lace
curtains to oblivion.

CD sales were down and dropping prices
worked on some, but baskets meant
to be full remained empty
and hurried shoppers dabbed
at red clay, performing delicate
maneuvers back to their
cars, locked against migrant thieves,
up from the south on holiday.

The Psychology of Elvis

Elvis would be plagued by memories of glorious nostalgia during his entrapment in Kansas. His eyes, so often reflecting the lights of Las Vegas, would sparkle again only during his dreams. Glitz, showgirls and excitement would spin his head. After awakening, he would pull the drapes open in his Topeka motel and be shocked by reality: empty streets, cold storefronts and a legislature debating intelligent design.

Vegas Memories

oh no, not again, he's
stuck, stinging his pride,
but straddling
monster fences
must be evil,
nowhere to go, but down.
his loud voice brings
cheer and oatmeal; leave it to
meg and mark to bring
his songs back
from Hawaii where the roiling
waves seem creamy and slippery enough
to move people right and left,
no one suspecting
lyrics to be
anything at all
but ciphers, their tunes teasing
men to bask in valleys,
their beliefs running up traces
of smoke and disappearing
in skies of black and blue.

Burning the Elvis Files

records going back ten, twelve years,
each photocopy pleasing music historians, yet
the records of love are not kept, but destroyed.
Why?

if each paper weighs its impact
on a golden scale, no one cares
but scavengers of the heart,
so—?

clear the slate and start
counting backwards, hoping
your conscience falls asleep
and you can regain
those paper losses,
only paper, not your soul,
not to be loosed upon the fire
some warm day beyond
assignations of regret.

We lust for knowledge.

Perfumed Love Notes

if hearts could wait
so tenderly in repose,
waiting near cash register's
mournful electric drone,
the totals ripped from codes
of honor,

if lovers could halt
their storms, those broken bottles of
remorse, fragments scattering
the perfume of love notes
past the slithering aisles
of acceptance,

if those long sighs could cease
their moaning, soft echoes
of wet kisses on lips
rejoicing entwinement,

if ghosts of lovers' laughter
tinkling from harps could only
spin forever
in the heavens of cool evening's
quiescence before fermenting
into doubt.

Chasing the Blues

all too splendid in memory
events telescoped elongated.
traversing blue-eyed couples dancing,
their shoes shined by elves poking
rags of ivory under and around knots,
while tap-dancing fairies rushed beyond
gated communities sheltering domestic
flowers found in baskets
from the Nile.

all converge on Beale Street,
with ink blots registering tired
blues singers blown
off course, cruising
the curbs looking
for deep-fried catfish
and Zydeco honeys, topless in their
dreams, making horny language
with silk tights and bow ties.

Dorothy Waving, Waving

she seemed distant, a far
off dot of pretty, a red dot
of not purity, but of a
freshening in the ozone, one who
marched rather than walked,
a flotilla all by herself,
waves of blue ocean caught off-guard
by eyes steaming with originality,
one vein pulsing in her neck as she
pushed through crowds, waving
one hand to fend off
tiny strangers wearing less than chic,
her other arm grasping the small hand
of a child, a tugboat in
distress.

The Emotion Begins

I first saw Elvis Presley on the ED SULLIVAN SHOW on January 6, 1957. When he sang "Heartbreak Hotel," he was so different and his voice so compelling I was shocked. We lived in Toledo, Ohio, at the time and I was a senior at St. Francis de Sales high school. It was a vital moment of recognition for me of his talent. I've been a fan ever since.

Heartbreak Hotel

blanched beyond white, visitors staggered
into the restaurant, ignoring place settings
for the moment, simply stunned.

each one aghast in robes of black,
effortless or legless in
their movements, whipping sideways down narrow
aisles huffing now, losing
their aplomb entirely, their
tired cowls dropping off heads shaved
for discipline.

fruits sliding into jello,
mountains of mushrooms awry,
each monk mystified by habits
malformed by choir-boy years, music
misheard by congregations
poised for soup, not eager
for salads.

still they came, buses revving engines
outside while mincing predilections for ambrosia
lingered on faces stern with rebuke, exhaust
fumes sucked in by air conditioning.

the chopsticks never arrived,
these utensils replaced by cold blades
razor-thin, splintering grapes in two,
hacking at marmalade, depositing caviar
onto plates steaming with
ravioli.

would no one notice
and stop the chorale before it
loomed too close for enrichment?

Visiting Oz

the carriage shimmered in heat
too surreal for yellow brick roads, and
counting horses as they glided by
our table made up for
tears of use.

no Wizard whipped gaily, each horse
kept step easily, with lathered
hips grinding through smog.

daily events like these
upset most tourists, used to service
without distractions.

one plum pie served
with ice cream, one large dollop of potato
salad on a bun, three waitresses taking breaks
off the rear exit, their lit
cigarettes glowing brightly
in the steam heat.

wine poured, yes, but why,
since the delicate glasses were chipped
by vagrant dishwashers hiding
in dark cellars?

from far away they came, eager
for American life, no
photo identification
needed, but customers
smirked at accents
deep in excuses.

would they be fired tonight?

Shotgun Bungalow in Tupelo

for this experiment, take off
shoes, socks, get off the chair,
sit down.

scrunch small, then
turn, lie down and use your old
legs to push.
that's it.

now push hard until
you're looking up
beneath the table.

remain calm.
take a deep breath.
get under there,
all the way.

night's traffic-flickers
cast mystery, don't you think,
about the kitchen's walls?

elaborate preparations should decline,
just lie there,
take deep breaths, and
watch the ceiling
with one eye,
then close it,
use the other,
go back and forth,
first one eye, the other,
one eye again, back and forth slowly now.

the mood should hit you,
the mood of a playful kid,
waiting for magic.

any loud noise should shake you,
shake your faith in
god.

look up,
close your eyes.
the lights are out
and you are all alone.

Kansas Morn

the due date pulsed with rhythm
and fog spilled over dandelions, the entire
backyard full of craters.

night's glow hummed, energy commanded
the lady bugs to wake, not one
flying now, just hanging
from blooms, bedding down.

most neighbors shuddered, counted
their memories, the deep white
fog not lifting yet, the early morning
factory whistle ready to pop.

but cars cranked up, coughed, and workers
slipped inside, checking for mice.

early spring was like this
then in Kansas,
no one ready for super highways,
no one itching for a fight.

The Old Pink Cadillac

look out now, roll the window
down, flutter your eyelashes
till they hurt,
grab a tissue and blow.

flinging past eyeballs, rocketing
like magical farmers' fields,
the rows of alfalfa, chugging like
pistons, your hand cupped
to make mournful noises
out the side vent of the Cadillac.

pause in reminiscence, capture
memories from high school, the journey
you took to catch red maple leaves
for scrapbooks moldering now
in garbage trucks,
parked in suburban landfills
waiting for mulch to thaw.

Mixing Memory and Desire

One of the most interesting "Elvis" movies was directed by Jim Jarmusch: the title is MYSTERY TRAIN. It has captured the Memphis angst perfectly: Sun Studio with visitors from Japan; Heartbreak Hotel with a "virtual" Elvis ghost; and an Elvis impersonator with a gun.

And the movie is split into three different stories, each involving a late night radio program which is repeated three times, sort of like GROUND HOG DAY another one of my favorite films. One song in particular is played, the greatest late night song of them all: BLUE MOON.

Late Night Radio

oops! the table just moved,
jiggling my arm, and the pen
scratched across white paper,
a jagged image leftover
from 1972 when the green Torino
lost its power to amuse, a snow drift
bopped its front side, interrupting
"Blue Moon" tooting so romantically
from late night radio WHB, rockabilly
a constant vibe back then,
but now the table's movement episode caused
Torino art to appear,
and framed it
sits above the piano
waiting for Elvis' visit
(he might need a ride).

Kansas Rain

garden plots wet with rain, morning
mist prevents mower's morning blast,
the tour of plant-life provides highlights,
yet mums decline, colors blend,
roses last hues are pink and
then bright yellow, the elephant ears fold,
not hearing much but tender drops of rain,
and above the roof the sky darkens before
we shut the door and retreat to windows,
letting the cold hard rain come
down in a gusty wind.

The Ache That Is

no one understands high school,
the loneliness after the last bell,
the hoping for contact,
that girl
in the far seat in math
so untouchable
that pain of separation lasts the entire
weekend.

not even the promised boiled dinner,
that old English recipe, can soothe you
where you hurt, can stop the aching,
the dreams provoked by the moody blue
melody heard down the hall
from orchestra practice.

but quiet streets and autumn
leaves in the gutter, somehow bleak,
somehow nostalgic, show this day
might be remembered, if you can
hold onto Elvis in your heart,
and walk with that girl all the way
home.

Shopping for Amps

when teasing
your hair in little ringlets,
catching gifts by surprise,
each catalog page thumps with electronics,
each page ramps with silver conduits, projectiles,
miniature cavities filled by wires,
early urges shopped
for gratuities so smooth,
the volume must be turned way up,
the notion of quiet
stunned by bass.

the urge to bark, or sneeze, so
many grotesque knobs to be turned,
to be shimmied,
headsets to be worn,
earlobes to be kissed,
pleasantries of excitation
rammed through credit cards and
easy access, till tomorrow
arrives and pulsing sensors
deplete sleep, eyes wide open
to the croak.

Mean Woman Blues

I'm not sure what was expected, what
I even wanted, her face so close to mine,
her hands tight, her grasp
on my wrist promising,
and I pulled back, not allowing her;
not inadvertently, as if she
might relax, her hold strengthened,
her nails drew blood.

what did she want?
I didn't know, I looked into green eyes,
the intensity there a brilliant orange,
the green-orange too much
for any man, cut wrists
burning with salt, each new
movement met
with a kiss, each new thought
stifled by her tears.

Running from the Ghost

I wasn't running away,
I knew the issues, really,
each one fermenting deep, and only
some unlikely conversation
might hold some rewarding emotion,
perhaps just a look
of understanding,
but the nightcap proved deadly,
the quiet so astounding, her
answer echoed for minutes,
and I opened the massive door,
bloodying my thumb on the lock,
slamming the door: intentional
you ask?
yes, but the night air
compounded the echo, and my
footsteps splashed along
the muddy alley, until
I turned the corner alone,
the shadows of souls
ratcheting roundly off bricks,
the old church chime
sounding oblivion.

Elvis and His Mom

I've always been intrigued by Elvis' relationship with his mother, Gladys. An only child, his twin dead at birth, Elvis should have been spoiled, should have been a mommy's boy with little masculinity. But he ended up brave and strong, but still with a big love for his mom anyway. He heaped presents on her, and carried on numerous love affairs too. How did he do it?
Was she tolerant of his affairs? Was she liberal? Was she proud of his conquests? Did she know about them? Did he hide them from her?

Elvis Waits for His Mother

mother was late, (She'll be here. Stop.)
after her noon tea at Paulette's,
soaking up too much chocolate,
no doubt, but we waited, and I
couldn't stop touching her,
she pulling away (Your mother, she's coming,
you know.) and I still held her close,
from behind,
running my index finger along her neck,
teasing her hair, inching my right hand
inside her black blouse.

but mother was late, late again,
and she removed my hand,
sat down in the rocker, pulled
her black skirt up,
teasing me with bare white skin.
(Don't do that, she mocked.)
What?
(Don't watch me, she grinned.)
but I stood behind her again,
touching her soft skin,
and we heard the car door slam.
(Your mother is home.)

she stood up, stopped the rocker,
held me close,
then went to the door.
(Say hello to your mother.)
hello, mother.
how was tea?

The Failed Lyricist

even the title portrays
another attempt at futility.

even the cautious words
splinter when mouthed.

falsifying brings eager animals,
the dogs of misplaced thoughts.

turning over the printed page
the writer smudges a vowel.

the light touch fails him, too,
nothing springs up dazzling.

hours go by and reviews
do not plunk in mailboxes
rusting in the snow.

A Reverie of Ants

after the rain,
the ants come out
in clumps.

homes ruined, they carry
tiny eggs, rolling them away,
avoiding puddles.

some insect buzzes with
an abacus, making sure
all are saved.

will another charge into
liquid mud, looking for babies or
will the sun scorch the nest?

the evening stills, but tiny
legs continue till
the morning dew.

Another Award Show

the supply is unlimited, names
dripping saliva, each one braying
at awards, wanting plaques and trophies.

some turn to dance, others
form roundelays, posing
near the cameras.

one more close-up is
demanded, and all
would fawn for fame.

let us praise these
hatchet egos, in love
with today, but smelling
tomorrow, when their
photos will bring them
joy, and impatience, eagerness
for much more ego-tripping.

Religiosity

Not all, but most of Kansas contains god-fearing, religious folk. Oh, they'll bring apple pie to you occasionally and they'll pray for you if you're sick, but mostly they're obsessed with low taxes, vouchers for christian (small c) school vouchers and sex prevention. Oh, and they fear they might have evolved from monkeys.

Because there must be no fun in Kansas and because you must be judged if you're bad, Kansans watch each other like red-tailed hawks looking for a kill. They elect ultra-conservatives who are afraid of sex, thereby, ironically, spending most of their time thinking about sex.

And their preachers tell them to ignore anyone else's opinions. Listening to new ideas might corrupt these poor true believers.

What they need (but won't admit) is a good dose of Elvis.

To Kansas Ignorance

oh to the brave non-thinker
reading no books or papers
who seems to grasp the essence
of pedestrian thought, taking in
word games off the net while
ruminating sin.

would all emulate this bastion of moral
fiber as he sulks in his tent of iniquity,
never willing to learn, never modulating
his iPod, but ever willing to pontificate
on moral matters, lopping off the heads
of evil-doers who flock to lectures while
reminiscing joy.

The Wizard Walks

about the knickknacks, above
the sink, he kept his stick,
wound with rubber bands for
a handle, it fit his hand like
a saber, rattling away when he
passed by the white picket fence.

no legal charge had he
for poking at people, no commission
of greenbacks or promissory
notes, no none, yet he
found targets: a Monarch setting south;
a boa constrictor basking
on a porch; a cluster of geese
primping wildly on the pond.

his feet carried him through
neighborhoods quiet with charm,
oozing with habitats, and his
stick protected him
from the visible world
while his imagination
wiped enemies
from his sight.

The King Explained: A Book Review

Thinking of Elvis Presley, if we ever think of him, may leave us with a
feeling of loss, of waste, of impossible success gone wrong, so very, very
wrong. In fact, Elvis might embody the very definition of a famous star
gone bad. He was the young revolutionary who lost his punch. He was the
virile, sex object who developed a paunch. He was the free spirit caught in
a pinch. In a word, Elvis Presley became effete, losing all of his energy, his
push for success, his love of life. Peter Guralnick (in his book, CARELESS
LOVE) has thought about Elvis, a lot, and seems to agree with most parts
of our definition of someone wasting his opportunity: he did have talent, he
did have great success, and he did throw away his life. Guralnick documents
three major problems that led to this waste: his manager, his fame and his
search for love.

First, Elvis signed a long-term contract with one of the most energetic,
but most egotistic of all managers, Thomas A. Parker, known as The
Colonel. At first, this contract seemed good, seemed lucrative. Elvis did
need someone to take charge of his life. After "Heartbreak Hotel," his
appearance on the Ed Sullivan Show and his romancing of the young
Priscilla who was underage for any sexual escapades Elvis might have in
mind, Elvis Presley needed someone who knew show business. He needed
someone to arrange his tours, his travel, his career. Such a man was Colonel
Parker (pp. 109-110). But the Colonel had a built-in problem: his ego. Sure,
he had experience in booking carnival and circus acts, but his ego, his
urge for his own success, drove him to ignore the needs of his client. Elvis
suffered, mainly because he was manipulated by the Colonel (pp. 151-152).
It is true that Elvis made a lot of money and kept his name in the papers.
But the Colonel limited his creativity, signing him to a long contract in
Hollywood where Elvis was forced to make absurd, quickie movies (p. 159),
made on small budgets (p. 152), keeping him on location for years, keeping
him away from live performances and his fans. The money piled up, but
Elvis suffered. He longed to get back on stage. The reviews for many of his
films were poor. "He is flat, he blurts out his lines, there is an almost total
absence of timing, conviction, commitment, tone" (p. 87).

Second, Elvis was so famous he found it extremely difficult to live a normal
life. Everywhere he went, crowds gathered. To meet his girl friends, he had
to have them secretly delivered to his home at Graceland. If he wanted to
see a movie, he had to rent the theater after midnight, and then sneak in.
Eventually, he became almost a complete recluse, having only sycophants as
friends (p. 270). These guys around him laughed at his jokes, reacted to his
every whim or idea as if he were a genius, and accepted his gifts of money
and Mercedes (p. 422), as if the presents were their legacy. Eventually,
his friends owned Elvis' brain, causing him to have an unreal view of life.

Sheltered by these friends and bodyguards, Elvis became very artificial and uncreative, lost in a world of drugs, sex and flattery. He was powerless to change his life since he could never stop being Elvis. Then, of course, one of his so-called friends decided to write a book about Elvis, a book that would reveal Elvis' bad temper, his use of drugs and his illicit romances. Such infamy bothered Elvis immensely (p. 608), since he was basically just a nice guy who been forced into an insane situation.

Finally, Elvis' biggest problem involved his love affairs, mostly with younger girls. We all know Priscilla was 14 and he was 25 when they met (p. 36). But she was not his only girl. Oh, no. There were Margit (p. 13), Dee (p. 14), Elisabeth (p. 15), Vera (p. 23), Nancy (p. 88), Sandy (p. 88) and so many others. Trying to juggle all these females was impossible. He would talk to one, sleep with another, meet another, phone a new one, and still try to be attentive to Priscilla. The poor guy just couldn't keep all these women pleased. He was careless with his love affairs, hence the title of Guralnick's book. They demanded his time and he had only so much energy. During his years in Germany, he had begun to use amphetamines (pp. 558-559), and he continued in the States. Often, this drug could keep him going, but with so many women and so little time, his system could never adjust. Pills, pills, pills. Sex, sex, sex. But no sleep. That became his lifestyle, a lifestyle that eventually killed him (p. 647).

The solutions to these three problems are, of course, moot, since Elvis died back in 1977. But since CARELESS LOVE is a cautionary tale, perhaps it might be worthwhile to give some advice to those who are going through similar problems today. The solution to the problem of an effective but domineering manager is simple: fire the man and get a person who really cares. But in show business, this action is difficult. Most managers are in it for the money. They want their stars to succeed, yes. They want their stars to stay healthy, of course. Obviously, a live star is better than a dead one. The Colonel saw all the signs of drug addiction and degradation in Elvis' life, but he didn't seem to care much. If Elvis showed up and did the gig, making millions for Colonel Parker, then that was the extent of his real interest. The Colonel made some attempts to "save" Elvis, but mostly he simply wanted money and control. Such managers exist everywhere in the music business especially. Musicians get dumped when they become unpopular. Musicians write songs and are given small percentages of the profits. The Colonel had a dream contract with Elvis, splitting everything 50-50. Most agents take 15-17 percent only. Elvis was being cheated, and he failed to fire the Colonel even though he had thought about it a lot.

The solution for fame is harder to solve. At first, Elvis and most entertainers are excited by fame and love the attention, the free women, the booze, and the travel. But it all gets old after awhile. Most stars attempt to build a bastion against the fans. Elvis had Graceland with a huge gate and fence all around it. But the fans camped out on the street all day and night for a glimpse of him. The photographers were always present. The tabloid magazines always needed a story, often not too concerned with the truth. If there is a partial solution to fame, it might involve using the fortune, the money acquired by fame, to ensure some privacy. With money, stars can travel to escape. They can hire bodyguards. They can hide, like Elvis, and only come out at night. But hiding and traveling are only partial solutions. The only definite break with fame is death. Elvis tried that, but his fame still grasps him to this day, with reported visual sightings in Memphis and around the world. Poor Elvis can't even die to escape the paparazzi. And only death stopped Elvis' interest in love and sex. "Ginger" was near him in the other room when Elvis went to the restroom for the last time and died in a puddle of vomit. How can a star learn to handle love affairs better? Using fame to lure women, Elvis could not be faithful to just one. His long-suffering wife, Priscilla and his daughter, Lisa-Marie, continually needed to adjust to Elvis' roaming. Perhaps his affairs can be attributed to the loss of his mother at an early age. Perhaps he was searching for someone to take care of him again. Maybe he merely liked sexual variety. But if fame allowed him so many lovers, the solution must come from Elvis or any other star's inner value system. Elvis believed in God, went to church, and sang hymns. He looked for help in psychiatric sessions and karate gurus, all to no avail. He loved attention. He loved women. But his life was a continual battle because of his affairs. He had a need for love that was unquenchable, and the one possible solution for others might be to increase self-esteem. Then, the star does not feel empty. Instead, the star feels good about himself or herself and can be self-sufficient. But, of course, there is no simple procedure to arrive at wisdom.

Elvis did have three basic problems that wasted his life involving love, fame and choice of managers. He alone could have solved these problems. If he had fired the Colonel and hired a more humane agent, if he had controlled the fame in his life by using his money to buy privacy, and if he had stayed faithful to Priscilla, he might be giving musical specials on television still, along with Shania and Ricky. He could have been the elder statesman of rock and country music. He could have been the model of good health and serenity, bouncing some grandkids on his knee. Instead, he died at 42, drugged out, desperate and degraded at the end, an ineffective, effete Elvis-impersonator.

Postcard from Memphis

once a photo, yellowing so,
could set the mind aglow,
bring back past deeds,
romance past needs,
and quiet the soul
enflamed by greed.

now instant brightness
captures all, the microchip
so current, no time
for thought or suet, just
take the shot,
don't talk, just do it.

Meth in Vegas

placate the enemy, hope you've
got enough change for the machine,
hurry cuz time flits by here
and no one knows
the depth, the height,
the length of fear.

After the Concert

the pumping never stops, the long lines
of cars, the toggle switches turned on
(Pay before you fill.)
the manager prods each car
forward, but no one moves,
each car blazing with static electricity,
each driver worried about oil
and how to spill it.

windows rolled up, kids in the backseat
bouncing rubber balls off
mom's head, her gum snapping inside
her head, her teeth grating, waiting
to get home, but no attendant
appears, no window washer comes out
with a smile for dad,
a rose for mom.

From Kansas, Claire Visits Memphis

We took our grand-daughter, Claire, to Memphis when she was nine. She knew I liked him and she sort of accepted him as a rather funny old singer, even while she teased me about him and laughed at the Elvis license plate on my truck.
But she was duly respectful every step inside Graceland, listening to her headset, observing every piece of history, counting every golden record on the walls.

Searching for the King

night walking through old neighborhoods,
I hear big cars squealing their tires, gunshots
ringing out at parked cars and babies screaming
for milk.

after midnight I slow down, each tennis
shoe frozen in goo, candy wrappers,
my old house alight with crack.

two persons jog away, plastic
baggies in their hands, cold vomit
retching up their throats.

my loud knock scares
the cat, the feline swooshing through bushes,
each eye aglow in yellow.

the lights go out, the TV too,
the people freeze. I'm just a haunted lover
wanting to go home, but afraid
to turn the key.

No one lets me in.

Fear of the Witch

we all have it, something fishy
sticking in our gums, a receptacle
filled with frozen steel, a current
touching bottom, like ice
water on a cracked tooth.

we all listen to it, heads
perched, a slight tingle in our receptors,
each knuckle cracking
with delight, each sinew bracing
in the night.

we all connect to it, ears
sweating boiled wax, each hair
twitching upright, sensors blinking
in our eyeballs, our feet steady at first,
then racing down alleys while
gunshots fly, and crooked
trees hide behind old barns.

Rats in the Cellar

behind the old records, Doris
Day, Lawrence Welk, the West Side
Story Soundtrack, somewhere in there
they hide behind the blue suede shoes.

but at night they can be heard
stuffing their bodies into walls,
creeping up to kitchens
lit up like someone's birthday,
and mamma forgot to put
away the peanut butter
crackers again.

the gnawing never
ceases till day-break,
but the traps clang shut on open
snouts and large feet,
the deadly pressure of the instant
snap popping up skulls, doomed now
as garbage, put out by the curb
for tomorrow's pick-up.

Rookery

Ann-Margaret was wearing something simple,
not a little black dress, but something clean,
nice lines, her shapely bod
fitting all the folds
nicely.

the others hoisted themselves
on stools, long legs promising
what? to whom?

and Elvis didn't mind,
pushing his way inside,
settling in a booth, red seats,
big table, his arms
outstretched to all
the ladies, their flashing
smiles warming him like
a covey of birds welcoming
a new egg.

Gig at the Bottleneck

suddenly he stopped, his music,
those effortless hits, warm and moving,
so silky as to be unforced, crystal
cool , funky, frizzy,
dominant yet subtle, raging
with poetry, bewitching, bewildering,
and finally, oh so tender, at night,
or at early dawn, one step away from sleep,
the dancing just went home.

Topeka Temptation

the distance between your door and the couch,
a few feet, and I can hear you
breathe, so softly, and I turn the TV down
to listen, my mind seeing your form,
under the covers, and my own breathing speeds,
the thought of me and you so close, the thin
sheet separating us, but my fingers feel
your shape from here,
and so I flick off the TV, stand up and
approach your bed, my clothes
slowly dropping to the floor, the beat
of my heart so strong.

Homesick

I suffer from real pangs of homesickness when I'm away from Memphis too long. I don't know why. I've visited maybe eight times. I've been through Graceland maybe four times. I've been through the Martin Luther King Civil Rights Museum about four times. I've walked the streets at night. I've seen Beale Street bounce back after years of neglect.

At the Mississippi riverfront at night, I've watched the city, the homeless sitting on benches, the quiet bulk of the water moving by, the feeling of something quite awesome in the air. And it isn't only my memories of Elvis. It's something much more. And Memphis isn't even my home town.

Missing Memphis

under the weather vane,
clicking helplessly, a small
chickadee, remote, lost,
but chirping vigorously, wanting
a bit of heaven, a bit of cold blue,
a wind to take him home.

Off into the Night

precious elevation,
the engines thrust,
only their lights seen
blinking, as the
powerful beast lifts off,
its passengers cuddling close,
or saying a few words
of calming patience, urging
the pilot up.

Night Flight to Memphis

below the sparkles linger,
an afterglow of traffic, each car
finite in a blur of white,
and each groupie relaxes,
readying for night,
the shear lace of stars above
calling their names, whispering
destinations, touching eyes
with infinity.

Remembering Indian Memorials

we call them primitive,
those original beasts in human
form, and they too mirrored the skies
with their imagination, hoping
for visitors from space.

their ancient rituals remembered
other visits, other gods;
the whirling disks came down before
and spread fire across the land,
their angel voices leaving
words and symbols
carved in caves, left behind
as guidance from the stars.

Ancient Thoughts on a Midnight Flight

the frightened men sighed
and played the game so ancient
and true.

they sought the laughter,
hoped for lyrics, waited as banter
led to vocalization; the light
voices charmed them and men
smiled with delight.

passages into caves led deeper,
and the damsels walked on,
ducking under stalactites and pausing,
winnowing grain for morrow, smiling
in remembrance and acceptance of their
male creatures, so slowly domesticating
at last.

The Memphians

noble riots caused by swelling,
first of extremities, then of gonads,
bursting loose, causing distant thunder,
the small group commenced toward
Bethlehem.

the urge for travel immense distances
but where in the world?
cucumbers quacked sound-bites, droll
green vegetation sprung up along the miles,
the walk became cumbersome, the overweight
eager for rest.

nostalgia filled their letters,
learned astronomers followed
their passage, noting drop in weight
and height, the gentlemen coughing
phlegm, and doing donuts in parking
lots.

but travel they must, and humping
to please they sent recordings of science
to the club back home near Graceland;
their mouthings made the "Hardball"
talk show, setting the nation abuzz.

The Elvis Mystique

Thousands of articles and reviews have tried to capture the essence of the Elvis phenomenon. And I've thought about it a lot too. The dying young and tragically is a big part of his allure. His obvious talent, and the waste of that talent. The hope that through all of his torments he might have survived. The hope that he still lives. The ache in the heart for him even now when we know he would be over seventy, not the young Elvis on the postage stamp.

I watched the Elvis parade in Kansas City in 2005: a whole host of impressionists, Cadillacs galore, and a fun-loving reverent yet raucous crowd watching the floats and cars and music glide by. Everyone was enjoying themselves. The sideburns and T-shirts and glitzy clothes were fascinating.

But what was it we were feeling? Was it his spirit?

Elvis Impressions

passersby nudged shoulders, urged iPod mates
to quench their listening, to wake up
and notice.

aluminum glowed red in the sun, its wicked
temperature busting elbow joints, the men
inside backing for art.

the red carpet rolled, some celebs mocked
each other, but the Impressionists stood tall
in their baking juice, the crock-pot effect
braising muscles, sinews.

Joli, Deneuve, Rampling, each to each
striding first, no brothers to kiss,
but miles of red coaxing them to seats.

How sweet to be embroiled in love and lust,
the big screen's exploits mimicked by Elvis mimes,
each camera poised to recall tidbits,
chocolate smudges on Joli's lips, her
smile wanton, her hot thoughts thinking
of poor Africans baking in tropical sunshine.

On Black Velvet

we need reminding, the time
clicking nervously, our feet in cold mud,
the answers found in retro bookshops,
only the keeper at the door
with enough time to cue.

we need the relaxation found
in tar pits, ancient animals lost
in ooze, their huge ears flapping,
then disappearing in blackness.

we need machines to rupture the cabal,
to excise the insects embalmed in translucent
amber, a reddish-pink disaster spanning
centuries.

we need artisans to pluck these bulbs
of taffy, to round them into ringlets,
out them on display in jewelry shops,
the asking prices pressed into velour napkins,
each courtesan advertising her own pleasure
moments.

we need time, we need sharing,
we need, finally, rest and beauty.

Bodyguards

relentlessly, the agent, his
computer skills honed on blaster games,
his sensitive skin attune with corpuscles
and centimeters, this man, yes, he took
over, searching through cache after cache,
looking through electronic symbols, those
erased seven magical times but still
pulsating somewhere, he was sure.

evidence, each citizen a suspect, each
finger click on keyboard suspect, yes,
each suspicious encounter
might tip off disaster, so
he was thorough,
seeking combinations, errors, faulty
decoding, willing to give
witness to computer crimes,
those crimes, he knew, could be traced.

Elvis lives.

Glamour: 1957

artists search for light
and find it near dusk when hot
pavement cools and robins
begin their night song.

certain men find it too,
their bodies lounging in open
cars, their radios playing
cool saxophones and musk,
their open collars relaxed, their
eyes searching for darkness
under the flowing trees.

women lingering on porches
feel the breeze, the touch
of evening's song; they fan
themselves languidly, their
eyes shadowed, their mood
curious and calm, the music
their invitation to dance.

TCB

the croquet mallets hit wood,
a solemn crack, the ball lilting
left, then right, near the wicket.

pale gowns let in the sunlight,
to women's bodies,
the lowering orb pinching
silhouettes between the trees,
its golden rays traverse the court,
the round balls blinking reds and greens,
while breezes move the leaves.

so gentle is the scene, no shouting,
no hurrahs, just a bit of mischief
and a sweet kiss.

Madison Avenue: 1958

sun glinting off windshields, the rush
of cars whipping past walkers,
the tall elm trees rustling with the cooler air,
couples follow the path; holding hands,
they breathe deeply, each one remembering
the distant early morning dew.

their walk slows, pauses, faces are searched
for smiles, and the moment lingers
in their souls.

darkness calls the children home,
the street quiets too, and the night opens
for the lovers, who find a park bench
to think of their tomorrows.

Golden Disks at Graceland

the gallery faded,
a blur, a phantasm, a mask
she allowed his eyes;
she accepted anything in this
flamboyant state, her mind
aflame with contradictions.

misty-eyed, she searched
the disks, first from afar
then closer, closer.

(oh, yes, her expert eyes
were swollen now, disk's blue-green
hue an iridescent blockage,
almost an inebriation.)

steadying herself, fingers
to wall, she wished for tears, but
none came.

such expertise she had
promised, but these fits mesmerized
her ego, forcing her to forget.

(often now she thought of windows,
opened to rain, to wind,
to disaster.)

leaving now, she closed his eyes,
rings of scalding orange
buffeting her brain.

(how could she return,
now that she had promised?)

but daylight brought back echoes,
those lightning sharp images
she knew, and black ink
would capture the staccato
guitar licks from memory's cave.

At Home with Priscilla

rustling leaves underfoot,
they walked, heads up, looking
through treetops, the lodge
a few miles off,
the moon so bright
they saw shadows on the haunted path.

each stop they talked, she
so excited by love, her green
eyes lit by yellow moon
dust, her hands clutching
for his.

they continued, some scudding clouds,
misshapen but in a hurry,
a storm whipping up,
and her smile the
only inspiration.

West of Memphis

warned of the evil, we
left the hut, our boots tied over our
jean cuffs, our hands holding
sticks,

a burnt charcoal smell
urging the dusk, we smelled
barbecue somewhere,
the cooler air
moving down the hill,
our camp far behind us.

we longed to climb, and
so we did, for thirty minutes,
each minute
bringing the sunset closer.

sitting on an escarpment,
we watched the broiling
orb lower so slowly,
we searched its meaning
for something timeless
past the turbulent Mississippi.

When the King...

when the King's mid-winter grasp
came out of its shell and
grabbed flying monkeys like it was
last Tuesday's sale on jelly balls,
the old stagehand rested a moment and began
to yodel, an art form lost on savages
but cradled by lovers on back benches of
tomorrow where grandmothers stayed
grandmothers and no one seized ransoms
for gobble-de-gookin' lip-synchin'
recording studios.

Believers at Sun Studio

take sacrifices now, if you read
your Bible you know
that handsome facial bone-structure
coupled with Octavian monstrosities
might equal fame.

just jump off the rat-trappin'
world for one minute and hose
down the backyard bubbles.

no one peeks into mysteries
better than a songwriter on beer,
each slobbering molecule resting
on mustache wax before slithering
down to mouths eager for cash.

Back in Kansas

Kansas City has the American Royal each fall. Here at Kemper Arena, folks from across the country get a taste of agriculture and cowboy life, with contests for everyone. Elvis would love it.

Part of the feel is America the way it used to be, before the Viet Nam War, before Watergate, before the Gulf War both One and Two. These are real heartland folks with excellence on their minds: church-going, healthy, outdoor people who know farm-life, livestock and the mechanics of the food chain.

But they are also the same folks who would hate the Elvis Vegas lifestyle and grit their teeth as Elvis gyrated his hips. For them, sex in the barnyard is fine. Mercy killing for animals is fine. But sex among humans—no, too unbelievable to be true. And killing your own grand-mother because she's in horrible pain because of cancer? No, let her die miserably, the way God intended her to die.

Elvis Rides Bareback

if the great divide splits
again, and water rushes down
the rivers onto the wheat fields
of Kansas, we'll see miracles,
we'll notice grandeur, and
the hoped for tragedies will poke
holes through geometry, while
winter-riders of noisy conveyances
will chuckle their yippee-yi-tie-yee-tommyhawks
again and chase buffalo
through the streets of El Dorado,
while Elvis rides the palomino
bareback one more time.

Surreal Drumbeats on the Plains

can't you just hear the thunder
in the snow, the storm swept plains bumping
loudly with misspent rocket shells, the flow
of the Flint Hills blocked by hard-charging
mounts, more Roman than the USA's
Fifth Cavalry, mounds of dirt flung up,
and soldiers carrying their dead back
to Abilene for burial, right next
to Eisenhower's farm, the blond brothers
smiling as their corn fields burn.

Retirement at Weston

each cello plucked its strings
and conductors readied their
hand-picked wands.

the silky moment over,
the brass collided with strings
and wilted dandelions perked up
to listen.

jumbled notes criss-crossed
attic floors on Main Street,
and no one moved much.

Now old haunted, Elvis rocked on his porch,
and the hot dog shop shut down
again, its mustard, ketchup, pickle
monotony turned to wriggles of yogurt
so youngsters could keep good
health inside.

a rap or two and the focused crew
drew breath and started again,
its July Fourth music tumbling
through the catch-basins of stale
Slurpies and older folks plugged
their ears, avoiding the deaf notes
of countless moles patrolling
the innards of the park.

When His Clock Stopped

what to do? it seemed all
new to customers usually so
attuned to nuance.

the creaking floorboards sensed
change and dimpled magazines
opened easily, revealing bathroom
features, closet-space-savers,
ratcheting pillows performing
with golden knobs.

another tick, then motion
inside, some people shuffling
toward drinking fountains, for
blacks, for whites, and children
were confused by colors,
when all they had were friends.

who to follow in line,
when teachers wished for
order and principals dealt
with disobedience gruffly,
raising wooden boards
to swat bottoms if the
time came again.

Elvis at the Writers Place

giving it a justification seemed
like sacrilege, but there he was,
at the back of the arena, the poets
readying their papers, a turbulence
in the air.

one man approached him,
wearing his White "Memphis" suit,
pointing to the dais,
his long hair greasy.
a smirk on his old face.

no groupies followed along,
he merely took a seat,
his smile
broader now as he
listened to quaint deliveries,
some sounding like the 1960s.

a grunt and he stood, reading
now, his guitar plunking some
vicious chords, his gravelly
voice mustering syllables,
some unknown, others
seeming to rhyme
before fading.

a poof of smoke, and the crowd
woke up, looking about, down
the long table, seeming
to hear but refusing somehow
to believe he was gone.

Puppet Villainy

toss out the jelly balls
and the fake coffee,
Cremora rippling on the cups.

such sticky things turn the puppets
and their porous skins into malcontented
beasts, each one complaining
in their boxes, each one refusing to jump
on stage when called.

but puppet meisters push tinsel wires,
capture pullied maneuvers, and scrape
up the flotsam of cushioned brains,
replacing entropy with ecstasy.

storyline's bravado cruises
audiences ready for laughter
and shellacked mouths breathe
sawdust, motions meticulous,
with lovers' wooden kisses
grinding pain from psyches damaged
by flat land's persecutions.

Paving with Yellow Bricks

useful capes flung in cement mixers
and Vegas pants pucker tightly,
butt's firmness revealed.

heat winds up from Wichita, asphalt gleams
with wavering mucous and craftsmen pause,
dripping sweat.

each brick coated with gold tincture,
each rectangle fits or is replaced,
tiny fingers fashion miracles until
dancing little people pluck their
eyebrows, throwing tap shoes each
to each, silver blades zing across the miles
and fields of corn shimmer in
August's heat.

Elvis Walks the Flint Hills

gossip tortures those famed by love,
their frames reduced to holding up
the past, their fingers itchingly erect,
as tumbleweeds from Oklahoma
direct flimsy attacks against the brave.

one figure, alone and fey, places his foot
on the hill, each step now a searching
for acceptance, and miles of sleek slake
outline the far Kansas blacktop, blending
darkness with the stink of tar.

motionless now, his heart throbbing
with loss, his mother's vision burping
up past traffic lights and stop signs,
his strength issues requests for gospel
songs, those sung in southern churches,
anything to distract his mind
from the sorrow of knowing sin.

The Capture of Elvis

flicking across the mind a vision
one of control, one of show business,
one of calculation.

headaches come late and sleep
is forbidden; instead, the pounding
of a mission, following the orders
of the colonel, afraid to disobey.

not many resist cash, cold and clever,
such manipulations, the movies so
glam, so weird now,
as we watch them after midnight.

who sponsored the man or
did he appear one day armed
with deceit?

but at night he reappears and devil's
tricks reveal the depth of danger,
the captured angel tormented and torn.

no soul could resists, and he hopes
only for love on someone's
borrowed couch, the beauty of the
moment washing away the tears.

BOOKS BY LARRY ROCHELLE

The Palmer Morel Mystery Series
Book One—Dance with the Pony
Book Two—The Mephisto Diary
Book Three—Cracked Crystals
Book Four—Trace Tracks
Book Five—Bourbon and Bliss
Book Six—Death and Devotion
Book Seven—Gulf Ghost
Book Eight—Blue Ice
Book Nine—Ten Mile Creek (Coming in 2007.)
Poetry
Dust Devils
Siren Sorcery
Pistol Whipped
Ghostly Embers
I Got Da Ever Lovin' KC Blues
Education
Prof Rap

Larry Rochelle was born in Toledo, Ohio, migrated to Kansas in 1978, and is
still trying to adjust to its extreme conservatism. Many doubt he ever will.
In high school, he began his appreciation for Elvis Presley and continues
his devotion to this day. His favorite Elvis song is "Moody Blue."
He believes he discovered surrealism as a poetic device after reading James
Dickey's poetry.
He is working on his ninth Palmer Morel mystery set in his home town
of Toledo, TEN MILE CREEK. It tells the tale of the remnants of the
notorious Purple Gang. It should be published in 2007.